MAKE MONEY NOW!™

MONEY-MAKING OPPORTUNITIES FOR TEENS WHO ARE HANDY

PHILIP WOLNY

ROSEN PUBLISHING®

New York

Published in 2014 by The Rosen Publishing Group, Inc.
29 East 21st Street, New York, NY 10010

First Edition

Library of Congress Cataloging-in-Publication Data

Wolny, Philip.
Money-making opportunities for teens who are handy/Philip Wolny.—
First edition.
    pages cm.—(Make money now!)
Includes bibliographical references and index.
ISBN 978-1-4488-9382-9 (library binding)
1. Repairing trades—Vocational guidance—Juvenile literature. 2. Building
trades—Vocational guidance—Juvenile literature. I. Title.
HD8039.R469.W65 2014
331.7020835—dc23

2012049003

Manufactured in the United States of America

CPSIA Compliance Information: Batch #S13YA: For further information, contact Rosen Publishing, New York, New York, at
1-800-237-9932.

CONTENTS

INTRODUCTION

On a quiet Saturday afternoon, while other teens might be at the mall or the park, one fifteen-year-old is busy earning money in her parents' garage. With money saved from allowance and birthdays, she runs a bicycle-repair business she established a year before. She started biking at an early age, and her father taught her basic bike repair and maintenance when she was only ten years old.

This afternoon, she has two bikes to work on and must update her bookkeeping for the previous week's work. She uses some tools borrowed from her parents and ones she purchased on her own, plus a free, downloaded spreadsheet program she taught herself. After finishing the day's physical work, she plans out the coming week: printing more flyers to hang around town; responding to queries on Craigslist, Facebook, and e-mail; and buying more supplies. She works most weekends and a couple of days each week after school, with more time during the summer. Ultimately, she plans to apply for a job at a bike shop with the experience she has gained.

Teens who are handy have many opportunities to earn money. Whether being their own bosses, earning wages at a local business, or even volunteering to gain experience for future work, they can pick and choose the path that suits them best. There are many types of work to pursue as well, requiring different skill levels.

Gaining experience through physical labor opens up a world of opportunity for those with the patience and talent to pursue such work. Earning money doing handy jobs is a great way to develop skills, problem-solving abilities, and discipline.

A young man examines a bicycle wheel on the job. Being handy can be a fulfilling and profitable path for teens, and it can prepare them for lifelong careers.

Teens who love to tinker with machines, or simply prefer working with their hands, also position themselves for various jobs, careers, and professions. These include engineering, physics, architecture, and other professions, as well as highly valued "skilled trades" such as carpentry, electrical work, construction, auto repair, and many similar vocations.

Even those who do not pursue these career paths have much to gain. They learn how to manage time and money, whether self-employed or as an employee, acquire valuable experience and skills, and get the satisfaction of earning their own money. Many teens love such work for its own sake, too. For them, fixing a simple household appliance can be as fulfilling as playing sports, writing a poem, or going to see their favorite musical artist in concert.

Learning about and preparing for these opportunities are among the most important steps in the journey. Teens must learn about the many local labor laws that affect them, learn to network and advertise, and perfect their job-seeking and interviewing skills. They should also learn how to handle money and clients or customers. At the same time, they must carefully consider what jobs they are ready to do, and how their work fits in with their plans for the future. Doing their best, they can enter the world of money-making opportunities for teens.

CHAPTER 1
A WORLD OF OPPORTUNITY

What does it mean to be handy? As the words imply, handy people are skilled in working with their hands. Their abilities usually go beyond just physical labor. Being handy means much more and can include many different types of work. Handy people are also known for being good with tools and machinery.

There are many reasons that working with one's hands can be a good choice for both the present and the future. In the short term, it is a great way to earn extra cash. In the long term, one learns valuable life and work skills that can be useful in many different career paths. These include a future in the skilled trades, such as being a mechanic, carpenter, electrician, plumber, and many more possibilities. Being handy also opens the door to other profitable and rewarding fields like engineering, computer science, and architecture, among others.

DEFINING "BEING HANDY"

Handy people may realize early on that they are especially good at doing physical and technical tasks. Even very young children can demonstrate a true love of using tools and figuring out how the physical world around them works. Just as young writers or artists may start out writing in their diary or drawing, a handy kid might be fascinated with taking apart a telephone or other common household item.

Some teens may find out they like these kinds of hobbies better than artistic or other activities. They may actually even love so-called creative pursuits, too. In fact, handy people also often show great creativity, imagination, and problem-solving skills through physical work. The two worlds are not exclusive.

Even if they may not pursue a skilled trade or technical career as adults, young people can use their special abilities to make money in many different ways. A good deal of them do not realize they have this talent until later in life because they do not try it out or do not have the opportunity. An insurance agent may realize at age forty that she or he loves woodworking and start a business making furniture, while an executive vice president might discover a love of repairing and maintaining table lamps.

WHY BEING HANDY IS VALUABLE

For those who have the talent and inspiration, being handy—and making some cash as a result—can be not only financially fulfilling, but also emotionally satisfying.

Although science and technology such as the Internet have provided society with great convenience and

A teenager drills a piece of wood in a shop class. Many young people first discover their love of hands-on labor early on, often in school.

connectivity, many feel alienated (or separated emotionally) from the work they do every day. While it is certainly not true for everybody, many workers feel disconnected from the technology that surrounds them today.

Some teens considering a future career may find the idea of sitting in an office cubicle or working in retail, for example, unattractive. As motorcycle mechanic and writer Matthew Crawford wrote for the *New York Times Magazine* in May 2009, "Working in an office, you often find it difficult to see any tangible [real] result from your efforts." The manual arts allow workers to feel a physical connection to their jobs. Many find the physical results—a finished table, or a working engine—very satisfying.

HANDY PEOPLE NEEDED, ALWAYS

Crawford also pointed out that although many jobs in the "knowledge economy" that numerous people work in come and go, physical jobs both skilled and unskilled will always be there. "Now as ever, somebody actually has to do things: fix our cars, unclog our toilets, build our houses," he observed.

In the last few decades, many jobs Americans used to do are now carried out in foreign countries, a phenomenon known as outsourcing. A customer calling to ask about his or her cellphone or Internet bill might speak to someone in a call center in India, for example.

If people need to fix a car, computer, or phone; have their house painted; or have a new kitchen or bathroom installed, they hire someone in their own town or city to do it. When a hurricane tears down thousands of power lines, skilled men and women must come in person to fix the electrical grid. Princeton economist Alan Blinder also told the *New York Times Magazine*, "You cannot hammer a nail over the Internet." Handy people's skills will always be necessary and cannot be outsourced.

A repairman fixes a power line damaged by Hurricane Irene in the Riverdale section of the Bronx, New York City, on August 28, 2011. Technicians who are handy will always be in demand, especially in emergencies.

Think of all the businesses, homes, and things that people use in the modern environment. Now imagine all the trades associated with keeping them running smoothly: plumbers; mechanics; carpenters; furniture makers; construction workers; electricians; masons; heating, ventilation, and air-conditioning (HVAC) technicians; and field service technicians for cable,

A teenager pushes a lawnmower through a yard. Handy job opportunities often exist nearby, if one knows where and how to look.

phone, and Internet lines. Making money being handy in one's teen years can lead to rewarding, well-paid careers that will always be needed.

A CHANGING ECONOMY

The Great Recession that began in 2008 in the United States and spread around the world left many people with fewer resources than before. People who once had hired someone to install a door in their home, clean their pool or mow their lawn, or do other basic jobs, suddenly did not have as much money as they used to.

Handyman-type tasks once performed by professionals were a luxury for many as the recession continued. However, such changes open up a door of opportunity for young people who are handy. A neighbor in one's town can perhaps not afford to pay a landscaping company to keep the yard trimmed and neat. But handy teens can step into this vacuum and start their own neighborhood lawn service. The same holds true for home improvement, automobile service, and other types of maintenance.

In better economic times, a person may simply throw out an old television, piece of furniture, or other household item and buy a new one. When money is tighter, a handy young person can repair such items for less than a professional service might charge.

A RETURN TO MANUFACTURING

Teens choosing skilled trades, manufacturing, and other physical labor may be in luck in the coming years. Alan Brown, writing for the American Society of Mechanical Engineers (ASME) in March 2011, cited studies that showed that a majority of American teens were uninterested in the manual arts: less than 30 percent were enthusiastic about such careers. Also,

A TALENT SHORTAGE

A 2009 survey sponsored by the Ridge Tool Company (RIDGID) revealed some teens' negative attitudes about potential employment in the manual arts. Ninety-four percent of 1,023 high school students between the ages of fourteen and eighteen said they are not interested in working in the trades. Out of that pool of students:

- Twenty-five percent of those said they are uninterested because they are not mechanically inclined.
- Twenty-four percent said they are not good at fixing things.
- Twenty-one percent said they would not consider a job in the field because they do not know enough about it.
- Fifteen percent said they don't believe there are opportunities out there.
- Eleven percent believe working in the trades is not cool.
- Ten percent thought that skilled trades were not high-tech enough.

[Source: "Survey of High School Students Reveals Careers in the Skilled Trades Are at Bottom of the List." February 4, 2009. Retrieved September 4, 2012 (http://www.bloomberg.com/apps/news?pid=newsarchive&sid=a1UYvWLy6qjo)]

fewer adults nowadays enjoy working with their hands, even at home as a hobby.

This bad news is good news for handy teens, whose skills will be more in demand than ever before because of a labor shortage in technical fields. For years, high school students have been losing enthusiasm for such work. Industry leaders blame the fact that vocational classes have been cut over time. "The problem with kids not pursuing a career in the skilled trades is largely because they are not introduced to it," said Mark Yochim, a plumbing contractor, in a 2009 press release from Noria Corporation.

Many young people see working with their hands as unglamorous, uncool, or beneath them. Fighting this perception can interest youths in the field, as can reminding them that these jobs can be as well paid and challenging as others. Darlene Miller, chief executive officer (CEO) of Permac Industries and a founder of Right Skills Now, a training program for teens, told the Minneapolis-St. Paul newspaper the *Star Tribune* in May 2012, "The perception that you go into manufacturing because you don't have talent is wrong…The truth is, it's quite the opposite."

BE YOUR OWN BOSS

One of the best things about being handy is the opportunity to be one's own boss. Handy teens sell their skills and abilities. They can set their own hours, working around their school and personal schedules. Valuable lessons to learn include time management, scheduling, and keeping track of money.

INTERNING AND VOLUNTEERING

Depending on how handy or accomplished someone is, that person might not find paying work right away. One way to "get your hands dirty" and gain valuable experience and skills is to intern or volunteer. A teen interested in bike repair might be able to get free training by volunteering at a bike shop in exchange for inexpensive or free bike parts, for example.

Various organizations, including community groups, charities, and religious organizations, might have similar opportunities for a handy teen to build his or her résumé. While giving back to the community, he or she can build confidence and skills that can soon result in paid opportunities.

ENDLESS POSSIBILITIES

Being good with one's hands opens up a world of money-making possibilities. Later, you will read about the things you need to think about before getting started and what to do while building a handy résumé. Tracking one's finances; becoming familiar with labor laws for minors, education in safety, and

A young apprentice does some welding at a workshop. Apprenticeships can provide valuable training and mentoring.

technical skills; and developing the habits needed for working for oneself (and others) are all important parts of the process.

Figuring out what to do is a good start. In an increasingly technological world, technical skills are in demand. Televisions, computers, bikes, and countless other items with working parts need repair and maintenance. Even jobs that seem straightforward benefit from a skilled worker—like painting, maintaining pools and yards, window washing, and cleaning houses. Someone

might spend an afternoon waterproofing a deck, fixing a toaster oven, designing and building signs for neighborhood customers, or cleaning gutters on houses.

When in doubt, figuring out what young people enjoy most will lead them to jobs and tasks that are satisfying, as well as lucrative. Money-making opportunities exist everywhere for teens who are handy. The only limits are one's creativity, open-mindedness, and imagination.

CHAPTER 2

WORKING FOR OTHERS

Getting a job is one of the most common and straightforward ways for teens to earn money. Handy teens have advantages over others who are uncomfortable with physical labor or working with their hands. Working for others, especially for an experienced and skilled boss, is an education in itself.

AROUND THE NEIGHBORHOOD

For someone handy, there are still many employment options out there. These may depend on where the person lives and how close and plentiful the jobs are—for example, right in his or her neighborhood. A teen worker who lives in a hot and dry region might apply for after-school or summer work in pool service. Workers as young as twelve can master brushing, cleaning, testing water chemistry, and basic pump maintenance. Looking up pool service companies online—some of which even offer courses and certifications in basic pool maintenance—is a good idea.

COASTAL EMPLOYMENT

The same job-seeking approach works for those who live near ocean coastlines, rivers, lakes, and other waterways popular with tourists and leisure seekers. Keeping in mind age and safety

A pool technician tests the water from a swimming pool. Depending on the region, handy work can often mean working outdoors.

restrictions for their age groups, teens should take advantage of local maritime (sea-related) opportunities. Beach and tackle shops may need help.

Others can go for positions at places that rent out boats and recreational vehicles, where they can get exposure to engines, basic maintenance, and other aspects of the trade. Yet another possibility is seeking work at marinas and docks, where tasks might include helping to clean and maintain boats, docks, and other facilities, or renting out equipment.

LAWNS, GARDEN, AND LANDSCAPING WORK

Wherever there are private homes, clients need lawn and garden maintenance, or landscaping. Although such a job may seem easy on paper, it is often physically demanding and requires using tools. In most cases, teens must be at least sixteen years old to operate power-driven (electric) tools like lawn mowers, trimmers, or weed cutters. Even underage teens familiar with such equipment from home use cannot be hired for these tasks. Such laws apply to many different workplaces and are meant to prevent injury (or death) to inexperienced young people.

A plumbing apprentice checks on some equipment. Note that she wears a safety vest, a must for many hands-on positions.

FIXING THINGS

Another job option is working in businesses that concentrate on helping customers and clients with mechanical repairs and maintenance. A bicycle shop, for instance, is a great place for teens to use and build their skills, especially if they are into cycling. Even a younger worker who may not be able to handle some of the more complex tasks (or cannot do so legally) can absorb useful experience by watching closely and asking questions.

Another similar job opportunity is working at an electronics retail store or repair service. Handy teens might have skills in both electronics and hardware and software and can build a résumé handling the interior components and user-oriented side of computers, mobile devices, televisions, stereos, and almost any other type of consumer electronics. One advantage is that most such positions do not involve the use of heavy machinery or other complex equipment that teens cannot legally operate. Much like working at a bike shop, another plus is learning under older, more experienced workers who can train teens in both the mechanical and administrative aspects.

CLIMBING THE LADDER

It may seem that younger, yet able, teen workers are at a disadvantage in such jobs, even if they are handy and intensely interested in the work. However, proving themselves able-bodied will often quickly gain the trust of supervisors and business owners. Teens who build goodwill and experience and stay at a job for a while—say, throughout their high school years—will receive promotions and raises and be able to handle more "adult" responsibilities and equipment as they hit sixteen and seventeen years of age. They also put themselves first in line for being hired when they finish school and are looking for full-time jobs.

SKILLED TRADES: FROM THE GROUND UP

In the skilled manual trades, learning and developing useful money-making skills takes time. As with retail or other service jobs, teens start at the bottom. A beginner carpenter—sometimes called an apprentice—for example, may begin learning his or her trade in high school, or on the job, but must usually wait until the age of eighteen to really start working.

However, teens can apply for construction work or other junior positions in the trades even if they are too young to perform the tasks of older workers. These can include simple jobs like carrying heavy loads, being in charge of tools and supplies, preparing materials, making measurements or doing calculations, and doing paperwork and bookkeeping. Workers under age eighteen often get their big break by helping out in the office.

Even a simple errand like visiting the hardware store can be educational. It familiarizes the employee with the names, uses, and prices of specialized equipment and supplies. By proving himself or herself competent at the bottom of the ladder, the employee will gain the trust and respect of older coworkers. Coworkers will be that much more likely to help the person along with training and more responsibility.

To gain as much information as possible, a novice worker should always ask questions such as the following:

- Why use one type of tape versus another?
- Why are these nails good for this type of job?
- How durable is this material?
- Why is this tool more expensive, and what is it for?

They should also engage the different types of older workers they encounter, politely interviewing people in different trades if possible. This is one great way to figure out what subcategories of the trades interest them most.

HARDWARE STORES

Another job possibility is working at a hardware store. If young people know about hand and power tools, paint, electrical supplies, plumbing necessities, and other home-improvement goods, it is a fantastic environment to earn cash and help others with their needs. Workers learn customer service, bookkeeping, and other administrative tasks, including how to use a store's computer system. Nowadays, these skills translate well to future jobs in any field and can provide a foundation for those who want to start their own business one day.

They can also greatly expand their abilities as salespeople and their knowledge of a wide variety of goods. Hardware stores usually reflect their geographical areas. A seaside town's store might have marine and boating gear, while one in a farming area will offer agricultural supplies. Hardware stores are central to any community, and workers can make good contacts with neighbors and customers. One financial benefit is the chance to get goods at a deep discount, or for free, for oneself or one's family.

An employee at a giant home-improvement and hardware store helps out a shopper. Jobs requiring hands-on skills may also benefit from providing good customer service.

GETTING THAT JOB: FIRST STEPS

Getting that first job requires some effort. Step one is putting together a résumé, the document that any job seeker must e-mail, mail, or submit in person that provides contact information, work history, and other important details that will make employers want to hire that individual.

A professional résumé will have a teen's work record, including personal accomplishments relating to the job applied for, and any relevant school coursework listed. For example, teens should include metal or wood shop classes they have completed and any similar training they have received from others and even any self-taught skills that show potential employers that they are handy.

To develop or improve a résumé, teens can consult parents or family members, check online for the many resources available there, and seek the advice of school guidance and employment counselors.

LOOKING ONLINE

Checking employment Web sites is crucial for job seekers. Online search engines allow users to find local job openings. Some well-known sites include Monster, Indeed, SimplyHired, Cool Works, SnagAJob, and USAJobs. The more résumés someone sends, the better chance that potential employers will respond.

Other resources include Web sites for local state departments of labor and the U.S. Department of Labor. Various public and private organizations and programs exist that specialize in promoting teen employment, too. Googling or directly contacting community-based organizations, religious and church-based groups, and other nonprofit organizations can provide leads. Cities and states also sponsor many youth employment programs, especially summer jobs programs,

THE MOMENT OF TRUTH: INTERVIEW TIPS

The following are helpful pointers when interviewing for a job:

- Be on time. If possible, show up early. Do a practice run from your home to the interview site beforehand, and plan the commute ahead of time.
- Dress professionally: neat and tidy.
- Get enough rest the night before. Seeming tired during an interview is a turn-off for employers.
- Bring a copy of your résumé; if possible, bring multiple copies.
- Arrive well informed about the company or business that you are interviewing with.
- Brainstorm questions you might be asked and their answers, as well as your own questions about the job and business.
- Be confident: look the interviewer in the eye, avoid nervous body language, and speak in complete sentences. Practice avoiding pause words such as "um" or "like."
- Fill out all application materials legibly and completely.

many of which include job training. It is a good idea to apply early in the year for programs that begin at the start of summer vacation.

POUNDING THE PAVEMENT

Teens should not only look online for jobs, but also visit actual places of business to apply in person. These include offices and stores, including both major chains and privately owned businesses. Options might include local construction companies and other businesses in the manual trades, retail and wholesale equipment sellers and repair shops, large chain stores that need handy employees, and many more.

Appearing in person—dressed appropriately and professionally, and with a positive attitude—shows bosses and hiring managers that a job seeker is serious and eager for work. They are more likely to remember a teen who shows up in person than the dozens or hundreds of applicants who only e-mail or apply online.

WHO YOU KNOW: NETWORKING

Networking is a crucial part of job seeking. A useful tip is the old saying, "It's not what you know, but who you know." That is why it is vital to keep eyes and ears peeled for word of openings from one's relatives, family friends, and even parents of friends or acquaintances. Teens should contact members of their professional or social network as often as possible to expand their employment possibilities.

Often, it is these personal connections that count, mainly because there is otherwise little difference among teen candidates for these jobs. All things being equal, a company will hire a son or daughter, or niece or nephew, of an employee or someone they know. For instance, local summer jobs in construction might be hard to get. Even someone handy might not convince a hiring manager that he or she is right for the job.

What you know is equally important as whom you know when it comes to being on the job, however. Lazy, clumsy, or incompetent workers who are unwilling to learn or have a bad attitude will not last long. They are easily replaced.

DRESS TO IMPRESS

Beyond just a résumé, teens should show up to interviews and places of business dressed professionally. This mode of dress

A job candidate who is positive, smiling, well dressed, confident, and professional is that much more likely to be hired when interviewing.

can mean a button-down shirt, tie, and slacks or pants for boys, and a skirt or suit and blouse for girls. In many cases, "business casual" is enough for certain summer or retail jobs—a tucked-in polo shirt and khakis, for example. Go conservative: avoid oversized clothing or sagging pants, clothes that are sexually revealing like short skirts, wild hairstyles, sweatpants or other athletic gear, and T-shirts and jeans. Even if the on-the-job dress code is very casual, job seekers should dress to impress.

CHAPTER 3

WORKING FOR YOURSELF

Getting work experience as an employee is important, but it is not the only option or path for everyone. In tough economic times, such as the Great Recession that affected the United States and much of the world after the financial crisis of 2008, jobs have been harder to find, especially for young workers. Becoming an entrepreneur (starting one's own business) is a great alternative way for handy teens to make money.

DO IT YOURSELF

Rather than waiting for work from others, do-it-yourself (DIY) teens create their own opportunities. They may already know how to maintain a bike; paint a wall; fix a television, computer, or mobile device; or build wooden shelves for their bedroom. They realize that the best way is learning by doing.

Just as writing, mathematics, or drawing get easier with practice, so does being good with one's hands. The better someone becomes at something, the easier it is to translate those skills into money-making opportunities. In many cases, it takes only a little bit of money for an industrious teen to start a small business.

FIGURING OUT A TRADE

Not everyone who is handy has a clear idea of what kind of business to start. Those interested in working with wood might

Entrepreneurial teens can apply their particular talents to the needs of neighborhood customers. Here, a young worker touches up an exterior window frame.

find they have a particular talent for making birdhouses, furniture, or custom-made chess sets or other games. A cyclist or skateboarder may try his or her hand at bike repairs or using paint and graphic design talents to design skateboards.

Whatever one's passion or talent, the resources to get started are out there. They exist online and in books and manuals that one can order, buy at a bookstore, or borrow from the library. Schools often have elective classes that can help students discover and develop their talents. If they have the means, parents can help by enrolling children in private lessons or even picking a summer camp that has classes in arts and crafts and similar disciplines.

With some free time and dedication, a mechanically oriented person can get much of what he or she needs inexpensively and often for free. Visit local business owners and other people in your area. Chances are that someone is throwing something away or that learning materials are just taking up space in someone's filing cabinet or closet.

As mentioned, the Internet has the easiest and largest collection of materials any handy person could hope to find. Online communities for engineers, mechanics, and many other types of tradespeople have countless free manuals, textbooks, and instructions available for legal download. All you need to get started may be just a click away.

DIGGING AROUND

If all else fails, someone who loves to tinker can buy cheap items at a thrift store or find items along the street on trash day. Yard or stoop sales can also be a gold mine for a handy teen. Basements, garages, and attics are great places to discover broken or forgotten furniture, toys, appliances, and other items to try one's hand at fixing or modifying. Always remember, however, that parents should always give permission first; they are usually better able to decide if something is safe to buy or take home.

GETTING STARTED

Many entrepreneurs start small. Imagine a young teen that began learning woodworking at age ten, inspired by his father, a carpenter. His first "jobs" were small, simple furniture items given out as birthday and holiday presents: foot stools and picture frames. Within two years, he gained the confidence and skill to make larger, more complicated pieces, like a chest of drawers or a dining room table and chairs.

FROM HOBBY TO JOB

With his parents' support, this teen decided to get serious and turn his hobby into a job. He began by using his fathers' tools and supplies. Using his computer, printer, and stationery supplies, he made business cards and flyers. He posted these around the neighborhood and on the bulletin board at school, and handed them out door-to-door. Thinking creatively, he put them in local shopping areas and near malls and asked other businesspeople, such as doctors and real-estate agents, if he could leave materials for their customers to look over.

Online, he sent e-mails out to everyone he could and asked his parents

A teenager uses a soldering iron on a computer circuit board. Tinkering with household items can build skills that can later be marketed to others.

and siblings to do the same. Taking good, clear pictures of his creations, he put up free advertisements on community and classified Web sites. He set up accounts on Facebook, Twitter, Instagram, and other social media networks. These networks helped grow his audience from only a few family members and friends, to hundreds of potential clients around his city.

GROWING A BUSINESS

There were limits to how much this teen could expand the business, however. Sitting down with his parents, they agreed that he would limit his work to a maximum of two or three hours a day and only three out of five school days, plus five hours a day on weekends. They all admitted that balancing schoolwork, other activities, and free time with his entrepreneurship would be best. During summer vacation, he expanded his hours to five days each week and took more orders.

With these limits in mind, he made sure not to promise customers too much, too soon. He kept his prices lower than a furniture store might charge and figured out realistic time-frames for filling orders. Customers were rarely unhappy with the finished product; he learned how to renegotiate prices and give discounts when necessary.

KEEPING TRACK OF MONEY

Early on, this teen craftsman also realized that he would have to keep track of his expenses and earnings. With resources like free, open-source software and books borrowed from the library, he taught himself some basic accounting and spread-sheet skills.

Under expenses, he made sure to keep track of all receipts for wood, paint, varnish, tools, and other purchased supplies, plus bus fare and other transportation costs. Slowly, he bought

In a wired world, finding and maintaining jobs and money-making opportunities will likely mean relying on online resources, including social networks.

his own tools so as not to rely on his father's. Paid and unpaid invoices were stored on a computer and printed and stored in folders. When he had the money, he took whatever extra courses he could to improve his abilities. Like many small businesspeople, he opened up a PayPal account because it was the best way for him to safely perform online business transactions, as well as a joint checking account with his parents.

WORD OF MOUTH

Much like getting a job as someone else's employee, making money as one's own boss requires networking. It actually requires more (and nonstop) networking. A teen landing a job can rest easy for a while. But a handy teen with his or her own business often needs new customers and business contacts to keep busy and earn more cash.

Some types of work require more networking than others. The furniture maker might gain enough clients to last him or her a long time. A freelance bike mechanic may need more customers per month or year and must continue to hustle for them. If you work for yourself, you will come to realize how much of your time and effort should go to gaining new customers. It also depends on how busy you want to be or how much time you can actually commit.

SOCIAL MEDIA

Like the woodworking teen described earlier, any serious young entrepreneur these days should have some kind of online presence. Facebook and other social networks are just the beginning. A quick video of fixing a bike, with before and after footage, uploaded to YouTube can be a great promotional tool, for instance. One idea is to maintain and update a blog that describes daily activities in one's field. It may just yield some

PROFILE: A SOUTH CAROLINA TEENAGE ENTREPRENEUR OF THE YEAR

Inspired by a grandfather in the construction trades, fourteen-year-old honor student Jerome Smalls, a native of North Charleston, South Carolina, was already helping his grandfather on jobs by age eight, according to a February 2011 story by his local paper, the *Post and Courier*. "My grandfather always taught me the value of a dollar," Smalls told local ABC affiliate WCIV. He later planted flowers, cleaned gutters, and cut lawns. Inspired by a summer camp for entrepreneurs, Smalls started his own company, HandyKid, in which he demonstrated multiple talents. A nonprofit group, Yes! Carolina, selected him as state representative to an entrepreneurship conference in New York City. North Charlestown's mayor, Keith Summey, even declared July 28 "Jerome Smalls Day."

new friends with common interests, but might also draw in new customers. Keeping up with what others are doing also gives teens new ideas and tips on how to improve their own work, including following the blogs of both older professionals and young novices.

CUSTOMER SERVICE

A satisfied customer or client is one of the best forms of advertising. Providing customers with extra business cards, flyers, and other promotional materials will make it that much easier for them to refer friends, family, and other colleagues. In addition, make it clear to them that they can always get in touch

A great DIY business idea is washing or otherwise servicing cars. With enough clients, teens can also enlist friends or siblings in a profitable neighborhood business.

for other work or if they have questions or problems with work already performed or with items they bought. Answer any e-mails or calls or texts as quickly as possible, whether they are from existing clients or possible new ones. Entrepreneurs who act fast show others that they are professional and eager for work.

NEIGHBORHOOD AUTO SERVICES

A popular and easy-to-start business is running a car wash, waxing, and detailing service. The cleaning supplies are relatively inexpensive, and nearly any urban or suburban area will provide plenty of clients. Assuming teens can get enough customers, it is also a good choice for two or more teens working together.

Another step is to add other auto-related services if someone on the cleaning team has the skills. These can include changing the oil and replacing fluids, filling tires with air, visual inspection, or stereo and speaker repair, installation, and adjustment.

OTHER IDEAS

There are many other ideas for starting one's own business. They can depend on many factors and a teen's personality. If the person prefers working home alone, he or she can repair or build items at home, like the furniture craftsman mentioned earlier. Others might enjoy working outside: garden and lawn care, pool maintenance, and other outdoor activities might be best.

Teens who prefer visiting customers in their own homes might perform repairs or other handy work by advertising that they do house calls. One idea is to market services to senior citizens, many of whom are homebound and cannot do such work themselves. Others might be good salespeople and sell their creations door-to-door or rent space at outdoor areas like flea markets to sell handmade creations.

AN ORIGINAL IDEA

Other entrepreneurs can make it big by thinking of a new, original idea. Marysville, Ohio, resident Hart Main started ManCans after realizing that he could make and sell candles for men. By age thirteen, he was filling three hundred orders every week for uniquely scented "man candles" with smells like sawdust, campfire, bacon, and "Grandpa's Pipe." He makes the candles using soup cans, designs his own labels, and deals personally with his label and packaging suppliers.

While his mother helps him with the hot wax, Main basically runs the company. As he told AOL.com in May 2011, he has considered being an entrepreneur when he grows up, rather than his original plan to be a lawyer. "I like the fact that I have control over things and can make decisions and see what's actually happening," he said.

CHAPTER 4

TRAINING, INTERNSHIPS, AND VOLUNTEERING

In today's competitive market, paid jobs can be hard to come by. Since 2008, unemployment has been high, especially in the United States. An Associated Press report in June 2012, based on findings from the U.S. Bureau of Labor Statistics (BLS), contained bad news for teen job seekers. Employment for sixteen- to nineteen-year-olds was the lowest since World War II. About 44 percent of teens looking for summer jobs cannot get them or work fewer hours than they want to.

In past decades, getting a summer job was a common rite of passage. Teens now face competition from older workers, including seniors, new immigrants, and unemployed college graduates. More workers and fewer jobs means that less than three in ten teenagers now hold summer jobs. Federal and state jobs programs, especially for lower-income teens, have experienced big cuts between 2010 and 2012. Those with better social and professional networks and experience often land jobs more often—and better ones, too.

WORKING...FOR FREE?

In this competitive landscape, handy teens looking for opportunities often must adjust their expectations. Internships and volunteer positions are alternatives to paid work. Internships are junior positions in companies, mostly unpaid, that help younger workers gain experience and connections. Companies often hire their unpaid interns as paid employees. This makes internships excellent for getting one's foot in the door.

Getting a spot in one of the growing number of training programs out there is also a way to gain valued skills. Leaders in manufacturing, skilled trades, and other physical professions are expanding these programs for young people because they are finding it hard to hire young, skilled workers. Participating in one often leads to paid positions, especially through school/industry partnerships that help place candidates who are handy.

VOLUNTEERS NEEDED!

Nowadays, money is harder to come by for many businesses and private and public organizations and institutions, including charities, community groups, and faith-based organizations. However, this makes it ever more important that they take advantage of the many teens out there who still need something to do after school or during the summer and are eager to learn, even if they do not earn a paycheck. It can be a win-win situation for both sides.

APPLY EARLY (AND OFTEN)

As with looking for paid work, teens should start early, especially for summer positions and slots. Begin searching online and in the community in the fall or winter, months before the positions start. Deadlines may be set months in advance, and candidates need enough time to prepare, fill out any paperwork, and get personal recommendations if necessary.

Volunteers, such as this teen using a bubble level, can learn valuable hands-on skills while gaining the satisfaction of helping others.

Teens with work or volunteer experience should ask employers and supervisors to write letters of reference, including current contact information. Applicants should not put all their eggs in one basket, so to speak, but instead try for many

LOOKING FOR A FEW GOOD WOMEN

Women entrepreneurs also promote hands-on professions to female teens. Young women are among the many people that the industry hopes will fill jobs opening up in the coming years as older workers retire, according to a May 2012 article in Minneapolis-St. Paul, Minnesota's *Star Tribune*. Sisters Lori and Traci Tapani left jobs in the corporate world to run their father's metal fabrication company. They visit schools and job fairs, encouraging women to enter the industry. Jones Metal Products CEO Sarah Richards also reaches out to girls. Many do not even think of entering the manufacturing sector, not realizing it can be fulfilling. She told the *Star Tribune*, "From the outside looking in, manufacturing seems old and dirty and slow-moving. In reality, it's quite the opposite [...] There's a feeling of 'I made something and it matters.'"

different opportunities. The more they research and apply, the better their chances of landing something.

BUILDING HOMES, BUILDING TALENT

Motivated teens can get training and experience working with their hands through many different programs and organizations, many of which give back to their communities. One famous nationwide and international organization is Habitat for Humanity, which accepts volunteers to help build affordable housing for low-income people. Teenagers who are age sixteen and older can work on house construction in their communities. Helping the less fortunate while getting hands-on building experience has inspired thousands of young people.

Youth volunteers belonging to Habitat for Humanity's annual Learn and Build initiative analyze materials and take measurements while doing basic carpentry.

LOOKING LOCALLY

Teens can search locally by starting online. Digging deeper, they can ask family members, relatives, and friends about churches and faith-based organizations with programs targeting their age group. Community organizations, either funded by charity or by local, state, and national government programs, also exist that sponsor training and volunteer opportunities that concentrate on skilled trades.

FIXING BIKES AND GIVING BACK

Recycle-A-Bicycle, based in New York City, runs three shops that recruit and train handy teenagers in bike repair and recycling. It offers high school students internships, including school credit, and other training programs, in which teens learn basic bike repair and maintenance. Old bikes are donated and restored and either sold inexpensively or given away, and volunteers can earn a bike frame and other parts with its Earn-A-Bike program. The program, along with hundreds of similar nonprofits nationwide, often works with city, local, and state governments and the federal government, as well as local schools, to help teens gain valuable skills, give back to their communities, and learn about environmental sustainability and riding safety.

Three young men work repairing bicycles at the Brooklyn, New York, branch of Recycle-A-Bicycle, one of many bike-related nonprofits throughout the nation.

TOOLS FOR TOMORROW

There has been a push lately around the United States to bring back job training in manufacturing. Despite the Great Recession, many manufacturers actually find it hard to fill skilled positions. Industry groups everywhere have begun to work with governments, schools, and communities to prepare today's teens for tomorrow's jobs. In July 2012, *Businessweek* reported on several such nonprofit programs.

One was Second Chance Partners, based in Wisconsin. One teen, high school junior Tara Britten, went from being a truant who was tired of classes, to learning welding, reading blueprints, and acquiring other skills and even got a job at a local firm while still going to school. Before Second Chance, as she told *Businessweek*, "Nobody would challenge me at the level I needed to be challenged, so it made me angry and bored."

Such programs are popping up all over. BuxMont Manufacturing Consortium, a collection of fifty manufacturers in Pennsylvania, also targets young people who are good with their hands. Another is Rockford, Illinois-based Nuts, Bolts & Thingamajigs, a partner foundation to the Fabricators and Manufacturers Association (FMA) industry group. For $59 apiece, it offers a manufacturing camp for teens who are ages twelve to eighteen. The weeklong program teaches them how to build a scale model of a wind turbine, along with factory tours and entrepreneur training. Twelve-year old Alex Marshall told the *Rockford Register Star* in June 2012, "It's not just sitting in a classroom, it's hands-on, and I like that." In 2012, the FMA offered similar camps in seven states, including an all-girl camp in Chicago.

As these programs grow, many industry leaders believe they could help bring back U.S. leadership in manufacturing. Interested teens should seek out these kinds of programs for training to prepare them for jobs with benefits after high school graduation that pay far better than starting positions in fast food or retail. Checking with high school career counselors, local manufacturers, and government agencies are good first steps.

MAKING OPPORTUNITIES

What if there are no openings in programs, nonprofits, or other opportunities in the area? Sometimes, you have to make your

An instructor (on the ground) watches trainees on a pole-climbing prep course for possible employment with a gas and electric company in California.

own. There are countless places to go and people to contact who might not even know they could use a motivated teen's help and expertise.

A young person experienced with audio and visual equipment might visit churches, community centers, and local meeting places like VFW halls or YMCAs to see if people need help with wiring or hooking up their meetings for sound or projection. They can charge very inexpensive fees or do it for

free, depending on the situation. Doing so every weekend can be a résumé-builder and add grateful contacts to someone's professional and social network. Word of mouth about one's work can lead to bigger, more profitable jobs. At the very least, one can gain experience and the satisfaction of having helped the community.

Taking a walk around the neighborhood, an intrepid teen might observe buildings, fences, or other property that need repairs or at least a good sprucing-up. Offering to paint old gray fencing, fix doors falling off their hinges, repair broken lawn furniture, and make other improvements are other options. Exchanging contact information with people a teen has helped also builds goodwill and can yield more opportunities.

PITCHING IN WHERE MONEY'S SCARCE

During the recent recession, cities and towns have had less money than ever to spend on necessities. Teens can volunteer their skills at local institutions facing severe budget cutbacks.

These might include the following: a teen's high school, libraries, museums, community centers, community gardens, senior centers, health clinics and hospitals, city day camps, recycling centers, and more. Possible jobs that might need doing could include rescuing old school equipment, replacing light fixtures, painting, refurbishing bathrooms and other plumbing, repairing laptops, and fixing wheelchairs.

START YOUR OWN CHARITY

Teens might research whether local charities provide some of these services already. If not, they can start their own by placing an advertisement and getting like-minded handy colleagues involved. They can pool their resources and divide up tasks according to their various talents.

They can give back to even younger children, motivating them to explore their own talents. This can take the form of one-on-one tutoring or training in manual skills. Weekly workshops or classes for groups of neighborhood kids can also be both fun and productive. Such teen mentors can develop their leadership and networking skills. Other ideas include building partnerships with established community organizations, churches, and civic groups. The lessons learned through these efforts are not just good for one's résumé, but also prepare teens for life, grooming them as teachers, managers, workers, and volunteers.

CHAPTER 5
SAFETY, THE LAW, AND ETHICS

Working with one's hands can be risky. Rules and regulations surround the use of tools and machines. Learning about safety and the proper use of equipment, however simple or complicated, are two of the most important lessons for handy teens, especially inexperienced ones.

Above all, one must protect oneself and others from injury or death on the job. All the money in the world will not bring someone back to life or replace a missing arm or leg. It is up to teens and their parents, as well as their employers, to maintain safe and healthy working environments, both on the job and in any work teens do. Besides injury, all of these parties must work to avoid falling afoul of law enforcement or committing any actions that lead to lawsuits or other legal actions.

Finally, workers should abide by ethical guidelines, both as employees and when dealing with customers, clients, or other people who depend on their work. Ethics are often defined by law and by a workplace's rules and regulations, but not always. Sometimes, they are simply commonsense rules that make sure workers deal with others honestly and fairly.

THE LAWS OF THE LAND

Consult Web sites that cover state and federal labor laws for minors (anyone under eighteen) for a complete list of jobs and activities that are prohibited for any particular age group. Different, and sometimes quite complex, rules apply for those under fourteen, fourteen- to fifteen-year-olds, and sixteen- to eighteen-year-olds. In many states, for example, there are specific rules for different age groups working on farms or doing other agricultural work, especially those who work for their families.

Teens working with and around automobiles might be limited to particular tasks, such as cleaning, changing fluids, or inflating tires on cars (but not trucks over a certain size), and

Family farmers—such as this man, left, and his nephew, shown here in Greensboro, North Carolina—often work under different rules than other workers.

are usually prohibited from operating or working near hydraulic lifts and other power equipment. The same goes for other fields that use power tools, such as carpentry, construction, plumbing, and waste management.

OLD ENOUGH?

All U.S. states have minimum age requirements for teen workers. In most cases, someone must be at least fourteen years old to work. Rules are often stricter for those under the age of sixteen. Federal and state laws also restrict how many hours a week, and at what times, a teen can work.

During the Massachusetts school year, for example, teen workers under the age of sixteen can work eighteen hours per week and only three hours each day on school days and eight hours daily on weekends and holidays. During summer vacations, they can work up to a maximum of six days every week and forty hours. Older teens can usually only work until 10:00 PM. Many laws prohibit those under the age of eighteen from working with specific types of heavy machinery, too. Researching these details is important for both teens and their parents before applying for any job.

SAFETY FIRST

Most employers or supervisors, especially those involved in physical labor, will know what safety equipment is needed on the job and will provide it. Still, one should always research these details by obtaining a thorough job description before starting work and make sure that the proper gear is distributed. Common safety gear and clothing includes safety goggles, ear protection, sturdy gloves, respirators, face shields and masks (for welding sparks and foreign matter), steel-toe boots, long-sleeve shirts, overalls, and fluorescent vests for work sites.

For teens running their own business, safety equipment and clothing may be a bit trickier. More research is needed, and they need to purchase or obtain this gear themselves, rather than relying on others. Parents and other trusted family members are the first people to ask about the necessary gear for any job or task.

AVOIDING TRAGEDY

Thousands of workers are injured or killed on the job every year. Some tragedies are unpredictable, but many are preventable, arising from carelessness or poor planning and preparation. Unfortunately, some companies endanger their employees (including older, experienced ones) when they ignore age limits for young workers.

The *Dayton Daily News* reported on the death of sixteen-year-old Damon Osgood in August 2011. Osgood was working with his father on the family tree-trimming and service business when his father accidentally backed into him with a front-end loader.

In March 2008, according to the Occupational Health and Safety Administration (OSHA), a seventeen-year-old worker driving a front-end loader at an auto wrecking business caused a concrete wall to collapse onto his fifteen-year-old coworker, causing serious leg injury. Neither boy should have been working at the yard, or operating such equipment, because they were under the age of eighteen.

Lynn, Massachusetts, construction worker Bendelson Chavez, seventeen, was killed after falling 20 feet (6.1 meters) to his death from a church roof while on the job. According to an official state report, Chavez had received no training or information in preventing falls.

DANGER ON THE JOB

In a May 2011 blog entry for the Occupational Health and Safety Administration, Assistant Secretary of Labor David Michaels stressed the importance of work safety rules for minors. Michaels said that young people especially were entitled to safe and healthy working conditions and to proper training when working with or around tools, machines, and other possibly hazardous equipment or chemicals. Teens should not be shy about asking questions or reporting unsafe conditions. He wrote, "You want to show your new boss that you're a great worker, you may not ask questions, or you may rush a little. And being new on the job, you may not feel comfortable telling somebody when you feel unsafe or a situation is dangerous."

DANGER: MEN AND WOMEN WORKING

Employees, their employers, and self-employed workers should be aware of many of the common causes and types of safety hazards and work to limit them as much as possible. Falling is one of the most common causes of death or injury, and painters, roofers, tree-service technicians, carpenters, and many others working high up must be mindful of its dangers.

Workers of all types must also be aware of electrical equipment, exposed wires, and other shock hazards. Operators of heavy machinery and vehicles, and those near them, need to stay sharp to avoid crushing or otherwise injuring colleagues.

Self-employed teens, who may be unsupervised much of the time, should also be careful when using hammers and nails and sharp items like sheet metal, knives, and other tools. Unplugging electric tools or items being repaired will prevent shock.

A recycling plant sanitation worker dons protective gear, including a hard hat and respirator mask, necessary tools in many toxic work environments.

KNOWING YOUR TOOLS

Depending on the job, you will likely use some kind of tools or equipment. Read all instruction manuals or packaging

instructions, no matter how simple a tool or piece of equipment might seem. Before starting work using anything, ask a trusted, knowledgeable adult for proper instructions about its use. Never use any unfamiliar or new tool for the first time without adult supervision. It might take several tries before someone is comfortable with new gear.

The same is true for the larger environment of the workplace or work site. Proper training or instruction in how to use and work around ladders, scaffolding, and other structures goes a long way in keeping everyone safe.

Ultimately, the greatest piece of safety equipment you have is always there: your own head. Be alert and think through every action and its consequences when doing physical labor. Safety also means never picking up anything too heavy to lift, keeping hydrated (especially in hot weather), and avoiding exhaustion. Teens should always alert an adult if they feel dizzy or disoriented, or if they are injured in any way, however minor.

"HANDY TEEN, KNOW THYSELF"

As they explore the various opportunities out there, handy teens will discover that being patient and knowing their limits is better than rushing and over-extending themselves. Taking on a job that one cannot perform is not only bad business but can also be dangerous. You might be able to fix someone's remote control, but that does not mean you can safely fix a malfunctioning wall socket. Taking stupid risks can end up in embarrassment and can even be life threatening.

Instead, a step-by-step approach will yield the best results. Taking the time to build skills means starting small and climbing up the ladder. This is important not only in one's own private business, but especially if one works for others. It is arguably even more necessary in physical and skilled labor because such money-making opportunities leave little room for error.

Of course, one will make more mistakes at the beginning of the journey into the hands-on workforce; you will find that this is both expected and necessary and one of the main ways to learn. As a worker learns and gains experience, that person will obtain better-paying and more interesting work.

KEEPING THE BOOKS, LEGALLY

Teens doing any kind of work must also abide by all local, state, and federal tax regulations that apply to them and make sure to file taxes every year. Employees will have any applicable taxes taken out for them from every paycheck. They should save their pay stubs and make sure to get a W-2 every year for every employer they worked for. It doesn't hurt to review deductions with parents to make sure that all the numbers add up.

Self-employed teens will have to figure out their own payments, which are owed to the government as a self-employment (SE) tax. Keeping all receipts or records of any money spent as overhead for the business is crucial, as is tracking all incoming money. In most cases, income earned in cash must be tracked carefully, too. Checking with parents and government Web sites, and even consulting an accountant or tax lawyer will help working teens figure out their income reporting responsibilities. It is not worth the risk to get into trouble with the law. In some cases, someone who hides his or her income can also put clients and customers at risk.

A construction worker in a hardhat and safety vest holds a stop sign to direct traffic. Proper safety management on work sites prevents occupational injuries.

Along with safety, a dedication to ethical business practices and willingness to work hard are necessary prerequisites for handy teens.

BEING ETHICAL AND FAIR

Working teens should also be mindful of others in everything they do. In the workplace, this means taking responsibility for mistakes or failures and not passing blame to others. Bosses and coworkers rely on workers doing their jobs correctly. Being dishonest can even lead to accidents or injury for others, not to mention causing employers to lose money or time. Dishonest workers might be fired and will thus burn some of their bridges for future work.

Self-employed teens must be honest and fair with those who rely on their work, products, and services. Always do what is agreed on, without cutting corners. Badly made furniture can break and injure someone. Overcharging for sloppy work or service will anger and disappoint customers. A bad work reputation gets around quickly these days, either by word of mouth or online.

HARD LABOR

The manual arts are not for everyone, even if people have the talent. Many jobs can be physically demanding. Years of working with their hands expose many individuals to occupational hazards. Certain repetitive motions done over the years are known to cause the painful condition known as carpal tunnel syndrome. The risk of injury, exhaustion, aches, pains, and other symptoms of physical labor are also things to consider. Those with physical limitations should also think about how these limitations can affect their career progress.

The benefits of being handy, however, far outweigh the dangers of pursuing this lifestyle. Millions of people have found that the manual arts are good for their souls, as well as their bank accounts. Handy teens will gain discipline, independence, and satisfaction from money-making opportunities that are just around the corner.

GLOSSARY

APPRENTICESHIP A work arrangement in which a novice worker learns a skill or trade under an experienced practitioner.

BLS Abbreviation for the U.S. Bureau of Labor Statistics, the federal government agency responsible for tracking employment numbers and trends.

BUSINESS CASUAL A dress code in professional or business environments that, while neat and presentable, is not as strict as that of formal business attire.

CONTRACTOR A person in the skilled trades that agrees to a contract with a client to provide labor or other services.

DIY Stands for "do it yourself," describing a self-reliant philosophy of working or making things.

ENTREPRENEUR A person who starts his or her own business.

ETHICS Principles that guide the behavior of individuals and groups, including business relationships.

FRONT-END LOADER A wheeled construction vehicle with a mechanism attached in front for scooping loose material.

HVAC Abbreviation for heating, ventilation, and air-conditioning.

INTERNSHIP A working arrangement in which a novice worker, often unpaid but not always, receives practical training in his or her field. Internships are often taken by students who have yet to complete their studies.

INVOICE A formal bill or record for goods or services provided, stating the amount of money owed.

KNOWLEDGE ECONOMY Also known as the information economy, a loose term that describes many office-based jobs where the products are information and other content, rather than physical products or items.

MANUAL ARTS Any creative activity involving manufacturing or the skilled trades.

MARITIME Of, related to, or next to the sea.

MASON A skilled tradesperson who works with stone or brick in construction.

METAL FABRICATION The industrial process of changing the shape and nature of metal.

OSHA Abbreviation for the Occupational Safety and Health Administration, which regulates worker safety and health in the United States and is a division within the U.S. Department of Labor.

OUTSOURCING In the context of the labor market, the process by which companies obtain labor and service in foreign nations, rather than domestically.

SCAFFOLDING Temporary structures put up on the outside of buildings to support workers and equipment.

SE Abbreviation for Self-Employment Tax, the money owed the government by teens or other taxpayers who work for themselves.

SKILLED TRADE A trade or craft that involves manual labor in which someone receives specialized training, developing abilities over time.

TANGIBLE Describing something real that can be touched or held.

VOCATIONAL Refers to occupation or employment and specifically to a type of education that prepares students for a job in the manual arts.

W-2 A form that an employer must send to an employee and the Internal Revenue Service at the end of the year. The form reports a worker's annual wages and the amount of taxes withheld from his or her paycheck.

FOR MORE INFORMATION

**AFL-CIO (American Federation of Labor/
Congress of Industrial Organizations)**
815 16th Street NW
Washington, DC 20006
(202) 637-5000
Web site: http://www.aflcio.org
The AFL-CIO is the largest federation of labor unions in the United
States and runs scholarship and internship programs geared
toward those entering the manual trades.

Canadian Apprenticeship Forum
116 Albert Street, Suite 812
Ottawa, ON K1P 5G3
Canada
(613) 235-4004
Web site: http://www.apprenticetrades.ca/en
The Canadian Apprenticeship Forum provides services to youth
seeking to enter skilled trades.

Habitat for Humanity International
121 Habitat Street
Americus, GA 31709
(800) HABITAT (422-4828)
Web site: http://www.habitat.org
Habitat for Humanity offers teens volunteer opportunities to
gain construction skills while helping build homes for the
disadvantaged.

Job Corps
200 Constitution Avenue NW
Suite N4463

Washington, DC 20210
(202) 693-3000
Web site: http://www.jobcorps.gov
Job Corps is a part of the U.S. Department of Labor and offers youth
    job training in various fields.

Junior Achievement USA

One Education Way
Colorado Springs, CO 80906
(719) 540-8000
Web site: http://www.ja.org
Junior Achievement (JA) works to connect young people to jobs and
    careers.

National Youth Employment Coalition (NYEC)

1836 Jefferson Place NW
Washington, DC 20036
(202) 659-1064
Web site: http://www.nyec.org
The National Youth Employment Coalition advocates for and
    partners with businesses and government to promote youth
    employment.

Nuts, Bolts & Thingamajigs

833 Featherstone Road
Rockford, IL 61107
(815) 399-8700; (888) 394-4362
Web site: http://www.nutsandboltsfoundation.org
Nuts, Buts & Thingamajigs is the foundation of the Fabricators &
    Manufacturers Association (FMA) and provides training and
    promotes education in the manual trades for teens.

Skills Canada

294 Albert Street, Suite 201

Ottawa, ON K1P 6E6
Canada
(877) 754-5226
Web site: http://www.skillscanada.com
Skills Canada encourages and supports a coordinated Canadian
approach to promoting skilled trades and technologies
to youth.

Small Business Administration (SBA)
409 3rd Street SW
Washington, DC 20416
(202) 205-6600
Web site: http://www.sba.gov.
The Small Business Administration (SBA) is a U.S. government
agency that supports entrepreneurs and small businesses. Its
Web site includes resources for teens.

YouthBuild USA
58 Day Street
Somerville, MA 02144
(617) 623-9900
Web site: https://youthbuild.org
YouthBuild is a national organization, partnered with the U.S.
Department of Labor, that assists young people ages sixteen to
twenty-four in skills training. Participants in the program help
build low-income housing.

Youth Employment Strategy/Service Canada
Canada Enquiry Centre
Ottawa, ON K1A 0J9
Canada
(800) 935-5555
Web site: http://www.servicecanada.gc.ca/eng/epb/yi/yep/
newprog/yesprograms.shtml

Youth Employment Strategy is the Canadian government's initiative
to help youth with skills training, career development, and
summer employment.

YouthRules!
U.S. Department of Labor
Frances Perkins Building
200 Constitution Avenue NW
Washington, DC 20210
(866) 487-2365
Web site: http://www.youthrules.dol.gov
The U.S. Department of Labor oversees rules and regulations covering
all workers. Its YouthRules! initiative seeks to promote positive
and safe working experiences for teens.

WEB SITES

Due to the changing nature of Internet links, Rosen Publishing
has developed an online list of Web sites related to the subject
of this book. This site is updated regularly. Please use this link
to access the list:

http://www.rosenlinks.com/MMN/Handy

FOR FURTHER READING

Beard, Daniel Carter. *The American Boy's Handy Book: What to Do and How to Do It, Centennial Edition.* Boston, MA: David R. Godine, 2010.

Chylinski, Manya. *Manufacturing* (Ferguson Career Launcher). New York, NY: Ferguson Publishing/Facts On File, 2010.

Downs, Todd. *The Bicycling Guide to Complete Bicycle Maintenance and Repair: For Road and Mountain Bikes.* Emmaus, PA: Rodale, 2005.

Facts On File Editors. *Construction* (Discovering Careers). New York, NY: Ferguson Publishing/Facts On File, 2010.

Farmer, Lesley. *Teen Girls and Technology: What's the Problem, What's the Solution?* New York, NY: Teachers College Press, 2008.

Geier, Michael. *How to Diagnose and Fix Everything Electronic.* New York, NY: McGraw-Hill, 2011.

Harmon, Daniel E. *A Career as an Electrician.* New York, NY: Rosen Publishing, 2010.

Hasluck, Paul N. *Metalworking: Tools, Materials, and Processes for the Handyman.* New York, NY: Skyhorse Publishing, 2011.

Hindman, Susan. *Carpenter* (Cool Careers). North Mankato, MN: Cherry Lake Publishing, 2010.

Koenigsberg, David. *Handyman's Handbook. The Complete Guide to Starting and Running a Successful Business.* New York, NY: McGraw-Hill Professional, 2003.

Marsico, Katie. *Auto Technician* (Cool Careers). North Mankato, MN: Cherry Lake Publishing, 2010.

Masters, Nancy Robinson. *Heavy Equipment Operator* (Cool Careers). North Mankato, MN: Cherry Lake Publishing, 2010.

Orr, Tamra B. *A Career as an Auto Mechanic* (Essential Careers). New York, NY: Rosen Publishing, 2010.

Rankin, Kenrya. *Start It Up: The Complete Teen Business Guide to Turning Your Passions into Pay.* San Francisco, CA: Zest Books, 2011.

Senker, Cath. *Construction Careers* (In the Workplace). Mankato, MN: Amicus Publishing, 2011.

Teitelbaum, Michael. *Electrician* (Cool Careers). North Mankato, MN: Cherry Lake Publishing, 2010.

Tomecek, Stephen M. *Tools and Machines* (Experimenting with Everyday Science). New York, NY: Chelsea House Publishing, 2010.

Topp, Carol. *Money and Taxes in a Micro Business.* Greenville, SC: Ambassador Publishing, 2010.

Topp, Carol. *Starting a Micro Business.* Greenville, SC: Ambassador Publishing, 2010.

BIBLIOGRAPHY

Bainum, Stefanie. "Nothing Small About Teen Entrepreneur Jerome Smalls." ABC News 4/WCIV, South Carolina, July 28, 2012. Retrieved July 29, 2012 (http://www.abcnews4 .com/story/19138397/teen-entrepreneur-has-his-day).

Brown, Alan S. "Students Opting Out of Manufacturing, Trades—ASME." ASME.org, March 2011. Retrieved June 10, 2012 (http://www.asme.org/kb/news---articles /articles/early-career-engineers/students-opting-out-of -br--manufacturing,-trades).

Bureau of Labor Statistics. "Employment and Unemployment Among Youth—Summer 2011." August 24, 2011. Retrieved July 7, 2012 (http://www.bls.gov/news.release /youth.nr0.htm).

Butrymowicz, Sarah. "Push for Career-Technical Education Meets Parent Resistance." *Hechinger Report*, July 17, 2012. Retrieved July 25, 2012 (http://hechingerreport.org /content/push-for-career-technical-education-meets -parent-resistance_9015).

Courrégé, Diette. "High-Achieving 14-Year-Old Who Runs Business Called Handykid Is Named Entrepreneur of Year by Yes! Carolina." *Post and Courier*, February 28, 2011. Retrieved July 1, 2012 (http://www.postandcourier.com /article/20110228/PC1602/302289909).

Crawford, Matthew B. "The Case for Working with Your Hands." *New York Times Magazine*, May 24, 2009. Retrieved July 6, 2012 (http://www.nytimes.com/2009/05/24/magazine /24labor-t.html).

Driscoll, Sean F. "14 Youths Learn About Careers at
　　Manufacturing Camp at Rock Valley." *Rockford Register
　　Star*, June 19, 2012. Retrieved July 7, 2012 (http://www
　　.rrstar.com/news/x69096890/14-kids-learn-about-jobs-at
　　-manufacturing-camp-at-Rock-Valley).

Feyder, Susan. "Turning Manufacturing into Women's Work."
　　Star Tribune, May 12, 2012. Retrieved July 7, 2012 (http://
　　www.startribune.com/business/151187325.html).

Gralla, Joan. "Teen Unemployment Persists in Summer 2012,
　　as Teens Compete with Adults for Low-Wage Jobs."
　　Reuters, June 16, 2012. Retrieved July 8, 2012 (http://
　　www.huffingtonpost.com/2012/06/16/teen-unemployment
　　-summer-2012_n_1602254.html).

Klein, Karen E. "Worker Shortage? Teach Teens Manufacturing
　　Skills." *Business Week*, July 5, 2012. Retrieved July 20, 2012
　　(http://www.businessweek.com/articles/2012-07-05
　　/struggling-to-find-skilled-workers-manufacturers-target
　　-young).

McMaken, Linda. "How Teens Can Stay Safe at Work." *San
　　Francisco Chronicle*, June 20, 2012. Retrieved July 9, 2012
　　(http://www.sfgate.com/business/investopedia/article
　　/How-Teens-Can-Stay-Safe-At-Work-3650852.php).

Michaels, David. "A Letter to Young Workers: Your Right to a
　　Safe and Healthful Workplace." U.S. Department of Labor,
　　May 17, 2011. Retrieved July 21, 2012 (http://social.dol
　　.gov/blog/a-letter-to-young-workers-your-right-to-a-safe
　　-and-healthful-workplace).

Occupational Safety & Health Administration. "Young Workers:
　　You Have Rights!" OSHA.gov. Retrieved July 21, 2012
　　(http://www.osha.gov/youngworkers).

Shankel, Gerald. "High-Skilled Workforce Is Necessary for America's 21st Century Manufacturing." *Appliance Magazine*, August 2010. Retrieved July 22, 2012 (http://www.appliancemagazine.com/editorial.php?article=2360).

Shellenbarger, Sue. "Cupcakes and Cattle Breeding: Teens Turn to Summer Start-Ups." *Wall Street Journal*, April 15, 2009. Retrieved July 9, 2012 (http://online.wsj.com/article/SB123975649228419167.html).

Toren, Adam. "10 Business Ideas for the Teen Entrepreneur." YoungEntrepreneur.com, March 26, 2010. Retrieved July 9, 2012 (http://www.youngentrepreneur.com/blog/10-business-ideas-for-the-teen-entrepreneur).

Toren, Matthew. "10 Awesome Business Ideas for Teen Entrepreneurs." BusinessInsider.com, February 16, 2011. Retrieved June 25, 2012 (http://www.businessinsider.com/10-awesome-business-ideas-for-the-teen-entrepreneur-2011-2?op=1).

Wedell, Katie. "Teen Killed at Construction Site Identified." *Dayton Daily News*, August 15, 2011. Retrieved July 22, 2012 (http://www.daytondailynews.com/news/news/local/teen-killed-at-construction-site-identified/nMtQh).

Williams, Geoff. "ManCans' Hart Main: A 13-Year-old Entrepreneur Invents Candles for Men." AOL.com, May 10, 2011. Retrieved July 21, 2012 (http://smallbusiness.aol.com/2011/05/10/mancans-hart-main-a-13-year-old-entrepreneur-invents-candles-f).

Yen, Hope. "More than Seven in 10 U.S. Teens Jobless in Summer." Associated Press, USAToday.com, June 12, 2012. Retrieved July 7, 2012 (http://www.usatoday.com/money/economy/story/2012-06-12/teen-jobs-disappearing/55555506/1).

INDEX

Index

P

PayPal, 38
Permac Industries, 15
plumbing, 7, 12, 15, 24, 52, 55
pool maintenance, 17, 18, 41

R

Recycle-A-Bicycle, 48
résumés, 15, 16, 22, 26, 27, 28, 51, 52
Richards, Sarah, 46
Right Skills Now, 15

S

school counselors, 26, 50
Second Chance Partners, 49
self-employment (SE) taxes, 60
SimplyHired, 26
Smalls, Jerome, 39
SnagAJob, 26
social media, 4, 28, 36, 38–39, 43, 51
spreadsheet skills, 4, 36
summer jobs, 4, 18, 26, 28, 30, 36, 43, 44, 55
Sumney, Keith, 39

T

talent shortages, 14
Tapani, Lori and Traci, 46

training programs, 15, 27, 39, 44, 47, 48, 49
Twitter, 36

U

USAJobs, 26
U.S. Bureau of Labor Statistics (BLS), 43
U.S. Department of Labor, 26

V

vocational classes, 14
volunteering, 4, 15, 43, 44, 45, 46, 47, 48, 51, 52

W

waste management, 55
window washing, 17
women entrepreneurs, 46
word of mouth, using, 38, 51
W-2 forms,

Y

yard maintenance, 13, 17, 20–21, 39, 41, 51
Yes! Carolina, 39
Yochim, Mark, 15
youth employment programs, 26
YouTube, 38

79

ABOUT THE AUTHOR

Philip Wolny is a writer from New York City. He remembers fondly one teenage summer spent working in housing demolition, employed by his father, a certified electrician and occasional building superintendent. He is the author of another Rosen book on high-risk construction work.

PHOTO CREDITS

Designer: Brian Garvey; Editor: Kathy Kuhtz Campbell; Photo Researcher: Marty Levick